PHYLA OF JOY

PHYLA OF JOY

POEMS

Karen An-hwei Lee

TUPELO PRESS
North Adams, Massachusetts

Phyla of Joy.
Copyright 2012 Karen An-hwei Lee. All rights reserved.
Library of Congress Cataloging-in-Publication Data

Lee, Karen An-hwei, 1973-
 Phyla of joy : poems / Karen An-hwei Lee.—1st pbk. ed.
   p. cm.
 Includes bibliographical references.
 ISBN 978-1-932195-14-9 (pbk. : alk. paper)
 I. Title.
 PS3612.E3435P49 2012
 811'.6—dc23

                     2011048207

Cover and text designed by Howard Klein.
Cover photograph: "Tulip Back" by John Lehet (www.lehet.com).
Used with permission of the artist.

First paperback edition: January 2012.

Tupelo Press
P.O. Box 1767
243 Union Street, Eclipse Mill, Loft 305
North Adams, Massachusetts 01247
Telephone: (413) 664–9611 / Fax: (413) 664–9711
editor@tupelopress.org / www.tupelopress.org

Tupelo Press is an award-winning independent literary press that publishes fine fiction,
nonfiction, and poetry in books that are a joy to hold as well as read. Tupelo Press is a
registered 501(c)3 non-profit organization, and we rely on public support to carry out
our mission of publishing extraordinary work that may be outside the realm of large
commercial publishers. Financial donations are welcome and are tax deductible.

NATIONAL
ENDOWMENT
FOR THE ARTS   Supported in part by an award from the National Endowment for the Arts

For with You is the fountain of life;
in Your light we see light.

Psalm 36:9
New King James Version

CONTENTS

3

The world where I look for you
         is a world open
to other worlds without name,
a world where you are not,
         where I look for you.
                    —*Edmond Jabès*

Love doesn't sit there like a stone.
It has to be made, like bread;
remade all of the time, made new.
                    —*Ursula K. Le Guin*

1

YINGRI

Inside me is a bridge, or the beams of a house,
and an old ground swell beneath a garden boat.

Outside, on an acre of snow,
a winter sun, blinding.

PEAR-SKIN ZISHA

I am green in small groves,
      a shivering ginkgo

thunderhead,
      one intercalary moon

blossoming
      in our annual calendar

waxing and waning,
      cold spring eclipse.

You say evening prayers
      as I hum our names

across a cloud of kaolin and mica
      with a pear-skin tea set,

iron-mottled clay,
      hot *yixing zisha,*

porous melon. We rarely
      wash our earthenware

since tea seasons the clay,
      flavoring over time.

It is often said *zisha*
      eventually brews its own tea

as white, oolong, or green
      soaks the pear-skin stone.

Yes, reader of poems,
        our clay-infused words

unfurl tender book-leaves
        carved out of a hundred lines

singing this lowly earth
        to the fire-ash of our prayers.

Dear reader,
        in June you imagine

I love summer tea. Yes,
        I adore black pomegranate

and blessed orange pekoe.
        You are chrysanthemums

embracing a noon sun,
        oolong cup of silt

oswego, anise, rooibus
        or red-bush tea.

I sleep early at eight o'clock
        despite masala chai.

PRAYER FOR A BAMBOO-FLOWERING FAMINE

May we blossom every fifty years
without afflicting the people.

May our seed-pods nourish rodents
who roam our groves

without rebuking lands with famine.
May sweet potatoes and rice save us.

May ginger and turmeric flourish
to the bitter distaste of rats

while tresses of bamboo flowers
changeling white wasps

load the groves with seed
in rare perennial synchrony.

May our sisters flower en masse
hundreds of square miles apart

in the pale night. May our shoots
pray a silent vision of healing,

our rhizome-laden memories:
Yes, we share our hunger

only once on this earth, my love.
Let us bless our fruit and multiply.

DREAM OF INK-BRUSH CALLIGRAPHY

In prayer:
quiet opening,
my artery is a thin
shadow on paper —
margin of long grass,
ruderal hair, sister to this
not yet part of our bodies,
your lyric corpus of seed
in rough drafts of pine ash,
chaogao or grass calligraphy
in rough drafts of pine ash —
your lyric corpus of seed
not yet part of our bodies:
ruderal hair, sister to this
margin of long grass,
shadow on paper,
my artery is a thin
quiet opening
in prayer.

PRAYER OF RESISTANCE

How do we fly to heaven
with the resistance of weather?

Wedding gases, says a child.
No, they're noble gases

I say. No, they're wedded
to the substance of faith

as a sail eases far past trim
to an unseen edge.

To fly, we need resistance
says Maya, blessing a luff

of wing loaned to my first line
against the flow of electricity

in a voltage-to-current ratio.
When this goes wrong

the resistance we meet in life
winks at the universe,

a wafted prayer
where one hydrogen atom floats

in square miles of alpha forest —
where galaxies and quasars shine

before black holes swallow all
we remember since birth.

MEDITATION ON A CENOTE

I know the moon is a sealed water cave,
collapsed well where I sacrificed the self.
It was not a process of refined alchemy.

Calmly, with a carafe of blue hours
on my back, I swam miles to one mirror
where the undersea moon bathed

a circle of blotting paper on water.
The gray self, indiscernible from air,
waited in a silver eucalyptus grove

immune to rain, corporeal
in swift hills of mist or ruin.
I sloughed a wet gray dress,

quiet blue hours unfolding for breath.
Memory is a cenote or limestone pool
where the moon's underground eye

confesses fawn-colored vapor
or sublimates violet irises in a jar —
the self's watery other, shyly adrift

as the body: a cenotaph, water monument
for the self who is missing elsewhere,
empirical matter in a field of spirit.

PRAYER UNDER MESA LIGHT

Summer in the mesa chapel
wheels around unveiled heads,
drifts in white nests. Intercession.
One difference between the blind
and the sighted is this: Whether what is
already was. You choose which.
An eye for an eye or unmerited favor?
A likeness without shadow is this:
Love available not in part,
whole enough for you.

DREAM OF METASEQUOIA

Two o'clock is the weight of empathy.

A foot-washing stone, one foot deep.

Shards of clay once holding water.

Weight of light on the back of one's hand.

Cool stone where they lay down their clothes.

Cave under a flowering nectarine tree.

Quiet desert hillside in noon heat.

Holy water painted in waves and particles.

C equals the sum of a hundred dollars.

Weight of light not of ash or cool shade.

Two o'clock is the imprint of a petal or hand.

Weight across the eyes, dust cells of heat.

A room moves in direct sun for hours.

Weight of light in terms of braille.

It's worth a cast-iron stove or typewriter.

Pine cones, dawn redwood, metasequoia.

SUNDAY IS

A kind of raiment;
lifts summer screens
on Sunday, marriage
when it started raining
cochlea and inner windows.
A little water in a woman's ear,
Sunday's internal spaces of sound.
Quietly turn on a little prayer music.
Pray so love flows where none flowed.
Quietly turn on a little prayer music,
Sunday's internal spaces of sound.
A little water in a woman's ear,
cochlea and inner windows
when it started raining.
On Sunday, marriage
lifts summer screens,
a kind of raiment.

FIRE SEASON

June is set aside for naming the sighted woman.

Twenty-Nine Palms, Redwood City, Thousand Oaks.

I am the healed one, the one with new eyes.

Neither insurance nor spot fires burn miles north.

Three cities are named after women or local trees.

Santa Barbara and Santa Monica and Santa Ana.

Free-flowering saluensis and new florist's wire.

Jottings. Naming June for sight, not blindness.

June is the month of well-being for women.

Her pins are red lacquer, glass, paired rose.

Silk routes open in May. April runs her hand

over a new dress. Yellow citronella in pails.

Mosquitoes. Red denim flowers, one hand.

Lying on the couch with her feet up. April

grace is a form of love. Passing hundreds

of gallstones into a colander. One bitter stone

flames into a four-colored hummingbird.

SWEET GLOSSOLALIA

Bravura of light, one apostrophe.
Red flowers or commas in a square.
A blind woman types out letters twice,
costs a quarter per page yet too light.
Intraocular eye pressures are low.
Tuesday is lost outside a subway,
topographical map for the sightless.
Sun is a brown rose in a mineral spring,
rust-hued fossil of antediluvian tears,
myrrh burned in a true global flood.
Musical wind path for the blind. Madeira,
Brazilian river in paired confluence, tan blue
or amber-colored wine, nothing with tears.
She remembers typing out letters, honey
with a magnifying glass. Hot at two o'clock.
Potted tea sun. With scissors cut nopalitos
raining at the sink, thin as new hat pins
or tin silence on the wet cutting board.
Noon darkness salting a woman's eye.
Window shades. Eclipse for autumn.
White arms and leaf blindness, a typhoon.
Occasionally, dreams are inaccurate reports.
I open a letter. Open quietly, she says.
Tongues of flame, sweet glossolalia
of prophecies float on known languages.

PRESERVATION OF RARE LANGUAGES

Now and then, while writing poems,
we sense the Holy Spirit move us to pray
for the preservation of rare languages,
Zazao Papia-kristang Kanakanavu.

Old world tongues whistle in valleys,
school children chant geography
with sea birds on archipelagoes —
imperialists cast linguicidal shadows

across the land. As we pray, languages
are zephyrs, eddies of air, transparent
minnows, wind as an arm or breath
embracing to preserve *nag'iksapa*

on a three-inch nickel rosetta, a thousand
texts in one glass-marble-encased world.
Newspapers report one rare language
whose last soul, a woman, is dying

with no one around to interpret.
Others aren't so rare, divine
Aramaic of diaspora villages.
Clicking languages fade

after war or exile. Women
speak rare languages to children
keeping tongues alive, sounds
of domestic activities witnessed

by mosquitoes. *Nushu* women trade poems
bagged with rice or uttered in long lines.
A woman sees a poem grow like a melon.
How does a melon grow? After soft rains

on a vine, it bows under a knife.
A poem says its flesh sweetens sun,
firmness of syllabic melodies
past colonial phrase. In this century

thousands of languages will vanish.
Spoken words hover over a mouth
in the fading world of an octogenarian
woman with a flame at her throat,

lost alphabets or hieroglyphics carved
in wet clay, inked on papyrus, tattooed
wherever we live. We watch kitchen fires
yet carry well-water to our families

after a time of fasting. We are wedding harps,
a shawl thin enough to pull through a gold ring
after a time of fat melons and hummingbirds.
We walk home with hand-dyed batistes,

run up a flight of stairs, or no stairs on a hill.
We say the wealth of night is *te po i teturi,*
the round moon eclipsed as a syntagm
vanishes in a pool of oblivion

without sound
or light in this phrase
translated as this
or this…

PRAYER FOR HIMALAYAN BEES

Honeybees are vanishing.
Let us pray to save them
from wing virus, wax moth.

I float prayers in a tea bowl,
honey as *mi* on my tongue,
mi, the third tone in solfege.

A thousand shades of pollen
hum intoxicating rains
darker gold than bees

drumming at night to burn
a giant hornet out of a hive
one degree more or a cent less,

new inflation as the Dow falls.
Seventy-seven, seventy-eight,
paper currency weighs

nothing at the end of life,
blooms hapless in water.
Drowned bodies of bees.

Thinness to light, I imagine
my bone-angled shadow
passing honey without cost

to propolis, wax, and skin.
I lie down in blackberries,
raise silence in red clover.

What is the price of rarity?
An archivist whispers,
not dearth itself, rather

the rate of disappearance
and its inverse relation
to the abundance of desire.

ON TWELVE MINOR SEAS

> "The sea becomes the shore, the shore becomes the sea."
> —*Indonesian Proverb*

Salt of Sargasso Sea

No sailors
in sargassum,
sea of kelp.

Salt of Cosmonaut Sea

It is polynya,
sparse sea ice
nearly polar.

Salt of East China Sea

Internal waves
salt the tongues
of my ancestors.

Salt of Kara Sea

Radiological?
No one sees
the waste.

Salt of White Sea

North inlet
almost locks
winter ice.

Salt of Andaman Sea

Coral languishes
as algae migrate
to cooler waters.

Salt of Chukchi Sea

At a high latitude
the beluga
calve, feed, molt.

Salt of Yellow Sea

Fishing boats
of Huanghai
disperse light.

Salt of North Sea

Shallow or epeiric
sea on a shelf
in my hands.

Salt of Bering Sea

Water basin
of gray whales,
acres of cloud.

Salt of Arafura Sea

Wealth lies
in fishing nets,
prayers.

Salt of Aral Sea

Saline lake
vanishes

. . .

SONG OF FEMINARIES

exiled . a wire cage . penicillin-dusted insect . frail legs . *nüshu*
. women's writing . literally woman . book . written by women
. quivers in the cool . open current . I carry healing in my
wings . I recite . names of moths . phyla of happiness . she
remembers . alpha . imperial . pale green luna . or mourning
cloak . not *Lepidoptera* . feminaries . hand-bound . string . what
is the name . cyclicity . green chrysalis . butterfly lung on a
microscope slide . or vice versa . opaline . hydrophanous .
where only visible flowers . not hidden or budding . war .
feverish women . daughters . cut ones imported . medicine
water . sewn fragrance . russet-colored pear . swimmers . gold
existence . one of hundreds . in a series . signs for the blind .

PHYLA OF JOY

Yesterday

the lines of our hands
                delivered

new oleander, writing
a river boat in the field,

chairs and red leaves.
Our new lava

serves the fellowship
of today and century.

2

LOVE AND SOLVENCY

Lift your face. This is not poverty:
Associates see white shadows of illness
or transport. You have what you surrender:
Beaches of washed-up yellow forsythia,
white freesia and hyacinth lying in your arms,
a millionaire's liquidated assets blooming inward.
Love is a partial anagram for solvency.
Convalescence knows you possess
only what is relinquished. A tithe of light.

Monday is where camphor comes from. In parentheses, the camphor tree: simple as that. Men and women in the north watch for floods stemming from landslides. Every other day, a three-stringed balalaika is tuned in fourths. A man with a bleeding face jumps into a truck and drives away. A woman wraps remains of her white rose bush in white bed clothes. Hour on hour, a series of sightless noons. Camellias were brought from Asia to the West by missionaries. Invisible blue lines embrace the world, sightless meridians. If they're invisible, how do you know they're blue, asks a blind woman. A plane flies over pacific, mountain, central. Meridians over oceans, land mass, ice sheets. Sum of zero.

PRAYER FOR AN UNDERGROUND SUPPLICANT

Remember old flowers cast in your rustling arms,
liverwurst wrapped in newspaper, one blistering pound

or the moon's cracked birch bark
frail as a dollar on a blind woman's face, pale hydrangea

shredded and falling in rare archives, a paper subway
in a supplicant's underground darkness, swaying,

and a melanin-rich flower in this fluorescent tube
translocating water to and from unassailable air.

This is your graduated body, no ordinary
engine in the night.

PRAYER OF A XUEROU APIARY

In the blind woman's body,
thousands of gold bees arise

from their summer hive.
Bees burst out of scented flesh.

A word in my first language
is *xuerou*, blood-flesh.

Her spirit is a hive of words,
xuerou burned to air

while she prays,
lying on the floor.

QUESTIONS AND CANTICLES

The blind woman's tree attracts no vireos.

What mail do we have today, nine poems?

I can't remember the name of a woman, *azalea*.

Hundreds perish in a market fire on the outskirts of Asunción.

Paraguay River flows from Mato Gross plateau into Paraguay.

Late-blooming internal routes rarely confess love.

A young woman learns a new word, *ocotillo*.

Words for rice in several languages: *mi, arroz, riz, arista?*

Upright magnolia fruit, red fleshy arils, rays of blood.

Was this girl in a red dress born with a cleft palate?

Men and women learn how to build an aqueduct.

Soldiers and police dogs guard their dwellings at night.

Wednesday is seeds of the flower, one million.

HORSES OF FAMINE, HORSES OF WAR

Salvage all the stones, she said, and white scallions sprouting stiff winter wind. Her mother would listen to the radio, remember how a fight broke up a funeral in rain. The house of the man and his mute brother broke open during a spring storm. Sky peeled through a ruined ceiling, dark mold flowered in the walls, rain drummed diligently inside.

Horses of war, horses of famine.

Someone is passing on, she thought. She detected the bitter desire of a brown clove cigarette in the night. Or sweet desire to burn for the moment. A blind woman considered the inverted thinness of cigarette paper, almost fish skin or petal. A man is passing on and no one knows his name. Paper with a name on it floats out of her hand. A book is a closed green circle. Or a woman whose first name sounds like sycamore-fig whispered. Or a book is a shore. It encircles hungry fish consuming these words.

PSALM I

Thursday is cuttings of earth, cuttings of flesh as I walk past an open-air

tattoo parlor. A woman paints henna tattoos, red brown designs on skin.

Flower carpels and sepals, a dictionary in disarray. The blind woman

presses scriptural flowers into street hands. Spares change. Asks the

neighbor to tie up the bougainvillea shedding in the alley. Sounds like

a wedding, vibrant colors rustling asunder. Ties up the branches with

rope, sweeps the loose rogue scarlet of late summer, rough and wild, to

the occluded fence. Petals of truth and red sun. Uneasy cease-fire in

a war-torn city. Red earth and flesh burst open. Young stars are only

hundreds of millions of years old. God turns on the light in her body,

a soft lamp with a paper shade a mother uses while nursing her infant.

PSALM II

Sunday is water to wine.

You say, communion.

Zinfandel, not pure gin.

White zinnias?

No, wine, she says.

You said white zin.

White rain, petals.

Wine to water.

Or rain?

PSALM III

A yellow automobile appears in a sighted woman's dream, presages an aunt passing away, woman in a bias-cut dress. Memory no longer moors in the same. Or moves over the old irregular terrain. Open your eyes. Double strands of inheritance. Chirality. Our nucleotides are right-handed optical isomers. What is the probability of this in nature. Why carry this urn of ash, yesterday's blindness. An orphan in exile sketches a rose under a full moon. Chalk on tar paper, white eyes and petals enormous. Missing flesh, annealed bone, or memory of red butterfly knots. Hundreds of angels construct iron rails and wood ties pointing to the sky. Angels in denim work around an invisible clock. Relogio, this clock's aqua-colored hour. Satellites orbit the world's corpulent, blue-fruited well, transmitting the word of salvation with rayed panels.

PSALM IV

mesa
four-stringed harp

. . .
italic hills

blood-dusk
on peninsulas

where love is
a syllable

oasis of grace
this winter sky

capsized boats
praise

sin mantequilla
mahogany

confesión
montañas

rojo
forehead

salmo
aleatory

sings
curls blue-white

global flame
. . .

perfume
burns

shades
a hand

arroyos
tierra

hot stones
. . .

invierno
río

canto
selah

PSALM V

A young woman is raised by her four aunts.

In her mind's eye, love is a red purse or hibiscus.

What red wine, bitter tea, and hibiscus petals share in common:

I dreamed of tannin furniture, she says. Rattan chest of drawers.

Blood is healing medicine. Or a ministerial astringent.

Hunger as desire tempered by understatement.

FAITH BY HEARING

Phosphorescent hum
inherited only from mothers
passes from woman to woman,
source of fires paired and housed
by *ch'uang,* the ideogram for window,
studying books by the light of fireflies,
yin ch'uang, the light organ's inner cells,
filling the cochlear night with heard radiance:
yin ch'uang, the light organ's inner cells,
studying books by the light of fireflies,
by *ch'uang,* the ideogram for window,
source of fires paired and housed
passed from woman to woman,
inherited only from mothers,
phosphorescent hum.

3

INVOCATION

My body isn't shaped like a violin, said the girl.
Curve in my hip isn't deep enough, *profundo*.

One blue world, my curve vanishes.
You aren't a violin, said her mother.

Curve of my body holds no water.
No invisible meridians, the hours, divide it.

My body isn't a cup for a pear blossom, said the girl.
My hips hold neither fruit nor rain. *Succo dolce.*

You are not a pear blossom, said her mother.
You are not a cup to drink.

My body isn't a pomegranate or bell, said the girl.
I am not studded with crimson seeds or a clapper.

Your body is neither flora, fauna, nor brass.
You are not a mountain range. Our voices,

ringing as one, are not the boat-laden rivers.
We are neither rain nor snow. Speak. I am

my mother's daughter, four summers old.
I am a strong girl, fourteen summers.

Who is my father? Where is this man
to invoke a girl's image of noon?

Now a woman of forty years opens this letter
without the pressure of metaphors

invoking paternal shadows,
absent figures of speech, *veritas.*

HYACINTH SEA ROOM

The sea's fish-colored notes

    hum salt flutes to the late evening

      hyacinth in a room: wreaths of violet light,

        inland wavering space, a glass-cutter who fires

          tranquil eclosions of sadness, molten silica

            as a sea rolls within the iron earth's furnace,

              eight glasses a day for a body's minor salts

                drunk in potable blue affluence, wisdom:

              eight glasses a day for a body's minor salts

            as a sea rolls within the iron earth's furnace,

          tranquil eclosions of sadness, molten silica,

        inland wavering space, a glass-cutter who fires

      hyacinth in a room: wreaths of violet light

    hum salt flutes to the late evening,

  the sea's fish-colored notes.

IN PRAISE OF WASPS

for Hazel Ying Lee, first Chinese American woman pilot

Men who refused

to classify us as military

spurned our capacity to fly.

Christening with our names,

they secretly feared

the slender body, slim abdomen,

well-developed wings,

and often formidable sting.

Women's Airforce Service Pilots,

we transported military aircraft,

flew the open Stearman,

survived the wreckage,

manned the horsepower,

and embraced the swept-back wing.

SELENOGRAPHIA I

Softening in places, craterlets seen
on physical surfaces, felt skin
sleeps in the night. Not the moon

crossing a four-way street in pale nylons
swinging a chain purse, three-inch heels
and a flowered dress tied with a red belt.

Endocrine matrices of sweet maria
in her body, wrinkled azalea, pitted —
cooling dales, smattering craterlets

seen from here. No water for the loss
of weight in dry leaves, indehiscent
seeds closed at maturity, airless sea.

Teeth set, one cusp eroding the other,
she stands quietly on the corner, head
higher than the rising subway

shredding the moon lying in the arms
of a paper-shedding tree, eucalyptus —
lone selenographer with a telescope.

SELENOGRAPHIA II

In modest signs of age, awareness
shifts to skin, bones or oil for hair,
magnolia dust from a pouncet box,
raw nut butter of the shea tree, salve

mother of candles, she dresses lightly —
pain buds out of thin air, red spawn
blooms fevered matter with eyes,
the iron nectar of ancient meteors

experiences graceful senescence,
igneous knees, fire-formed
accents of the body, lunar soil —
youth flutters in a lost Rorschach

changing from ink moth to mother
with frail eyes — imago
searching for nocturnal pleasure,
water and glycerin on burns

misting the knees of a torsal volcano,
a root sweetens the beginnings of old
soap bark, bergamot, rosemary, almond
if her body metamorphoses —

for annealing, restoration of fissures
relinquishing self to holy fire, refining
a crystal vase of irises netted by heat stress,
losing flowers to flames, curled ash petals

singed by years of permanent waves, burns
assuaged by olive or castor oil, prayer
bleeds divine love to salvage myopia
strong as weathered lunar glass.

SELENOGRAPHIA III

A body's modest purse of hours —
Once a selenographer observed the seas
on the near side of the moon, in reality
covered with regolith, sparse dust hills

flecked with mineral grains, untrue maria,
canals and rivulets, streams or inner seas.
Maria are not literally seas —
fields of dark stone without wildflowers,

this maria not a body who emerges
from a tub of water, toweling herself dry.
Amateur selenographer with a telescope
breathes aquatic notions of the moon.

Is this the body observed without conjecture
dripping on the smooth rim of her personal sea
with whispering clocks of lunar craters
formed long ago when the world was

a thread of light in the beginning? Quietness
in her dust holds only what she owns,
memory, a body's modest purse of hours
and a minute amount of gravity.

SELENOGRAPHIA IV

Altered purity or visual density

for the aging process —

rate of wound healing

      flint and breccia

      bright oeuvre, leonides

a red moon

sign of latter times

      a blind woman dreams

      horses of war and horses of famine

lineaments of rage

      saturnalia and rivers in blood

      cubits high to a horse's bridle

winter ash

toxic fallout seed —

      lunar eclipse, newspapers

      incalescence

fear the war's dark fever

      density of a solar coronal mass

      light years in the universe

brush a magnetic field

yi shulian zai

a sunflower

      flares in the curve of a hip

her selenium deficient bone garden,

vigor in form of an almond flower —

SELENOGRAPHIA V

I pray slowly, opening alone
      to the aroma of amaretto

      eclipse
      the moon is red

a woman in a paper gown
awaits an examination

      looks into the potted dark
      solace of night in lunar soils

planes flame to earth
subways shudder to halt

      the moon wears
      sackcloth and ashes

a selenographer
      with a telescope
      spots satellites

refracted beauty of rayed craters
in lumens, solo flight.

TEA-PICKING OPERA

(right hand)

clockwise . a long circle . *mount jiulong* . a winding corridor . promise
to return . letter to circle . in the jubilance . paper umbrella . round
box with iron wheels . tea roasted to clarify the blood . one buffoon
. two women . linen aspirin or medicinal . uses of gold for the body
. open . *kangcha* . comic . right . nine tones . fan gesture . eighteen

(left hand)

counter-clockwise . *paocaicha* . tying a small basket . splitting the
salary . luminous thin . noctilucent sheets . in the clock . lenticular
cloud . sold tea to the wine seller . sublimation stirs . shoals . your
shining hands . left . river . specific gravity . laden . wedding
laughter . at the inn . sound one eye . left eye . rain . astir

CELADON STONE

I shield

a paperweight

     with my left hand.

Leaf on stone

celadon green —

     hand-glazed, it molts

a female glass dragonfly

alive to procreation,

     another life

on paper.

CELADON GLASS

A glass stone
        drinks the moon
chlorophyll pure —
floating on thin-leafed
        concentricities
of silent water,
ink and stanza
flow like wind on grass
        for my right hand,
transparent
        composure.

CELADON WATER

Is not ceramic,

jade, bone,

or sea —

it is old rain

drumming

in the wind,

one thousand

little stones

flown in a dream —

melting ice

or winter wheat

brushes my hands

while I sleep

on water.

CELADON PRAISE

Etudes of light falling —
copper rails of winter,
pear-white sun spears
split a room into letters
addressed to tender fields,
a daughter-in-law's
scriptural gold labor,
lessons of patience
weigh down lines,
love letters, prayers
still watermark fresh
under a celadon stone.

THEORIES OF THE SOUL

> "A true friend is one soul in two bodies."
> —*Aristotle*

Kant says, transcendental
    idealism. In Aquinas,

we exist apart from bodies
    but only on Thursdays

when his famous ox
    flies by the window,

wiser at Cologne
    where Albertus Magnus,

his real name, appoints
    Aquinas to *magister studentium,*

master of students. Aquinas
    is petrified but says *yes.*

He feels his soul
    sailing out of his head

floating near the roof
    where a blue ox wings by.

On Wednesday, two bodies
    are one soul

waking at sunrise
    thanks to the pineal gland

of Descartes, who thinks
    this node in the brain

is a tiny sugar cone
    or salted peanut,

the seat of the soul
    while Aristotle points

to the chopping ax
    as a teleology

as if the ax were a living,
    breathing person

which it isn't.
    Heraclitus, air and fire

while Aquinas objects, no
    not an ax but ox.

If you're a bird or soul
    I am only one mile

from the sea. If you
    are a soul in two bodies

life is more complex
    and we must labor

twice the field of sorrow
    after sleep, bath, and a glass

as Aquinas whispers, *the things*
    we love tell us who we are.

PRAYER OF NUPTIAL FLIGHT

The open river is thin as a poplar;
flower sellers lower their prices.

Certain insects sprout only once a year.
Shutting their wings, they stagger to the oil lamps.

Flaming down rainless mountains,
the summer has opened to the foehn wind:

an accidental lightness occurs.

NOTES

YINGRI

In Mandarin Chinese, *ying* may refer to the ideogram for shadow (*yíng*, third tone) or to the actions of reflecting, mirroring, and shining (*yìng*, fourth tone). *Ri* means sun.

PEAR-SKIN ZISHA

The title of this poem refers to a kind of teapot. The phrase *yixing zisha* refers to clay from the city of Yixing in China. When fired at high temperatures and left unglazed, this clay gives teapots a dark *zisha* color that I compare to the black-violet of California mission figs. "Pear-skin" is another way to describe the dark russet appearance of this pottery. "Melon" is a sister *yixing* teapot, where the *zisha* is mixed with other clays.

PRAYER FOR A BAMBOO-FLOWERING FAMINE

Every half century, the synchronous flowering of bamboo causes famine in parts of India, as proliferating rodents devour the bamboo seed-pods and then the crops raised by villagers.

DREAM OF INK-BRUSH CALLIGRAPHY

The word *chaogao* is Mandarin Chinese for rough drafts, literally "grass drafts." The poem also refers to the classical Chinese calligraphy script known as "grass calligraphy."

PRAYER OF RESISTANCE

Maya Lin is the architect of the Vietnam Veterans Memorial in Washington, D.C., the Civil Rights Memorial in Montgomery, Alabama, the Women's Table at Yale University, and (most recently) "What is Missing," a multi-locale, multi-genre memorial to species and places that have gone extinct or will disappear in our lifetimes. See www.mayalin.com/.

MEDITATION ON A CENOTE

"A cenote is a deep sinkhole in limestone with a pool at the bottom that is found especially in Yucatán." See www.merriam-webster.com/dictionary/cenote/.

PRESERVATION OF RARE LANGUAGES

The Living Tongues Institute for Endangered Languages inspired this poem. The Institute supports community-focused, multi-media projects for language revitalization. See www.livingtongues.org/.

PRAYER FOR HIMALAYAN BEES

For *Apis dorsata laboriosa,* the endangered Himalayan bee that produces intoxicating red honey.

ON TWELVE MINOR SEAS

An opening in an area of sea ice, a *polynya* is found mostly in northern seas. The lines "sparse sea ice / nearly polar" allude to this geographical formation.

PHYLA OF JOY

For the Kundiman Asian American Poetry Retreat, with love.

PRAYER OF A XUEROU APIARY

The word "flesh" in Mandarin Chinese is *xuerou*, which translates more literally into English as "blood-flesh." *Xue* is blood, and *rou* is flesh or meat.

PSALM IV

This poem arose from "calque" or words loaned from other languages. While some Spanish phrases are italicized in the poem, the loaned words — names for geographical features commonly recognized in southern California and the American Southwest — are not: mesa, montañas, río, and arroyos. One exception would be "canto" or song, un-italicized in tribute to the geography of a poem, where such linguistic migrations often take place. In the Spanish: *Sin mantequilla* means "no butter." *Confesión* is a confession. *Rojo* is red. *Tierra* is the land. *Salmo* is a psalm. And *selah* is a Hebrew word often found at the end of psalms.

FAITH BY HEARING

From Romans 10:17: "So, faith comes by hearing, and hearing by the word of God."

IN PRAISE OF WASPS

For Hazel Ying Lee, first Chinese American woman pilot. My deep appreciation goes to Judy Yung, author of *Unbound Feet: A Social History of Chinese Women in San Francisco* (University of California Press, 1995). Reading Yung's book, I learned about Hazel Ying Lee and the WASPs.

SELENOGRAPHIA IV

The phrase *yi shulian zai* refers to one who is expertly skilled in selenography, the study of the moon's surface.

TEA-PICKING OPERA
A tea-picking opera is a light-hearted, interactive Taiwanese musical drama, traditionally performed by itinerant troupes of the Taiwanese Hakka ethnicity, and typically including three roles: a tea-picker (the buffoon), his mother, and his sister. "Tying a small basket" refers to a basket thrown into the audience for cash tips or gifts *(paocaicha)*, gifts often used improvisationally within the drama. Tea *(kangcha)* was also sold at these performances.

CELADON STONE
The title refers to a sea-green transparent glaze often compared in hue to jade. This glaze originated in China during the period of the Five Dynasties (906 – 960 AD). This poem is inspired by a celadon paperweight, a little writing companion sitting quietly on my writing desk for years. It appears to depict a dragonfly and a leaf resting on a stone or, depending on the observer, drifting in water.

THEORIES OF THE SOUL
Thanks to the *Stanford Encyclopedia of Philosophy* for providing information about each philosopher and theologian. The final two italicized lines are credited to Thomas Aquinas. See http://plato.stanford.edu/.

PRAYER OF NUPTIAL FLIGHT
Once a year, on ant-flying day, male ants sprout wings and mate with the queen.

ACKNOWLEDGMENTS

Heartfelt gratitude to my loved ones, prayer warriors and guardians. Grateful acknowledgment is also made to the following journals, where a number of these poems first appeared, some in earlier form.

Another Chicago Magazine	"Questions and Canticles"
Beloit Poetry Journal	"Faith by Hearing"
Cairn	"Intercession"
Copper Nickel	"Dream of Metasequoia"
Crab Orchard Review	"Fire Season" and "Sweet Glossolalia" (as "Sweet Heteroglossia")
Crate	"Ounce of Camphor"
Dirtcakes	"Psalm V"
Ellipsis	"Yingri"
Emprise Review	"Meditation on a Cenote"
Fifth Wednesday	"On Twelve Minor Seas"
Iodine Poetry Journal	"Prayer of a Xuerou Apiary" (as "Prayer of an Apiary")
Iowa Review	"Prayer for an Underground Supplicant"
Journal of Feminist Studies & Religion	"Preservation of Rare Languages"
Melusine	"Invocation"
Mochila Review	"Nuptial Flight" (as "Aperta: Serrata")
North American Review	"Horses of Famine, Horses of War"
Poetry	"Dream of Ink Brush Calligraphy," "Prayer for a Bamboo-Flowering Famine," and "Theories of the Soul"
Prairie Schooner	"In Praise of Wasps" (as "Wasp")
Puerto del Sol	"Sunday Is"
Rosebud	"Celadon Stone"
Swarthmore Review	"Psalm I"
Tuesday Art Project	"Tea-Picking Opera" (as "Postmodern Tea-Picking Opera, Mount Jiulong")
Witness	"Psalm III"

"Dream of Ink Brush Calligraphy" has also been included in *Best Spiritual Writing 2012*, edited by Philip Zaleski (Penguin, 2011).

Tracy Estelle Tipton

KAREN AN-HWEI LEE is the author of *Ardor* (Tupelo Press, 2008) and
In Medias Res (Sarabande Books, 2004), selected for the Kathryn A.
Morton Prize by Heather McHugh and chosen for the Norma Farber First
Book Award by Cole Swensen. Her chapbook *God's One Hundred Promises*
received the Swan Scythe Press Prize, awarded by Sandra McPherson.
Lee has worked as a florist's assistant, mended books in a rare-book
archive, tended tissue cultures in a medical lab, read to children in a family
literacy program, and taught music lessons as therapy for mental health
patients. A former writing resident at the MacDowell Colony of the Arts
and the Millay Arts Colony and recipient of a National Endowment of the
Arts grant, she currently chairs the English Department at a faith-based
college in southern California, where she is also a novice harpist.

Other books from Tupelo Press

Fasting for Ramadan: Notes from a Spiritual Practice, Kazim Ali
This Lamentable City, Polina Barskova,
    edited and introduced by Ilya Kaminsky
Circle's Apprentice, Dan Beachy-Quick
Stone Lyre: Poems of René Char,
    translated by Nancy Naomi Carlson
Severance Songs, Joshua Corey
Atlas Hour, Carol Ann Davis
Sanderlings, Geri Doran
The Flight Cage, Rebecca Dunham
Have, Marc Gaba
Other Fugitives & Other Strangers, Rigoberto González
The Next Ancient World, Jennifer Michael Hecht
The Us, Joan Houlihan
Nothing Can Make Me Do This, David Huddle
Red Summer, Amaud Jamaul Johnson
Dancing in Odessa, Ilya Kaminsky
A God in the House: Poets Talk About Faith,
    edited by Ilya Kaminsky and Katherine Towler
Manoleria, Daniel Khalastchi
Biogeography, Sandra Meek
Flinch of Song, Jennifer Militello
After Urgency, Rusty Morrison
Lucky Fish, Aimee Nezhukumatathil
Long Division, Alan Michael Parker
Intimate: An American Family Photo Album, Paisley Rekdal
The Beginning of the Fields, Angela Shaw
Cream of Kohlrabi: Stories, Floyd Skloot
The Forest of Sure Things, Megan Snyder-Camp
Babel's Moon, Brandon Som
Traffic with Macbeth, Larissa Szporluk
the lake has no saint, Stacey Waite
Archicembalo, G. C. Waldrep
Dogged Hearts, Ellen Doré Watson
Narcissus, Cecilia Woloch
American Linden, Matthew Zapruder
Monkey Lightning, Martha Zweig

See our complete backlist at www.tupelopress.org

CPSIA information can be obtained at www.ICGtesting.com
Printed in the USA
BVOW08s2330290316

442244BV00002B/3/P